Ooh La L...
Activity Book

Calling all Moshling hunters! Greetings, Buster Bumblechops, super Moshling expert, here. Now, although I am fangtastic at catching these tricky little critters, I might just need your help today, because a few of them are proving more than a bit difficult to catch. Keep your eyes peeled (not literally!) in the pages of this book for Judder, Plinky and Oompah, they're teeny-weeny masters of hide-and-seek. Happy hunting!

Tyra's Sp...

OPEN

Can you also crack where I've left this Fried Egg Rug?

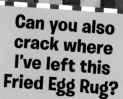

Ooh La Lane Quiz

Ooh La Lane, or should that be Lar-dee-da Lane? You don't have to be a poshi Moshi to meander down this lane, but it helps! Take in a bit of culture at the Googenheim, then pop into Tyra's Spa for a spot of monster relaxation.

1. What can you see through the arch in the wall between Tyra's Spa and the Googenheim Art Gallery?

2. How many vehicles are going down Ooh La Lane?

3. What creature sleeps on the wall near the Help Kiosk?

4. Can you spot the clock? What time is it in Monstro City?

5. How many sprinkles are there on the revolving ice cream on Guiseppe's Ice-Scream Parlour?

6. What are the three colours of ice cream on the revolving ice cream model?

7. How many potted trees are there outside the New Houses store?

Give this brain-tickling quiz ~~~ see if 'La Lane' is 'La place ~~~

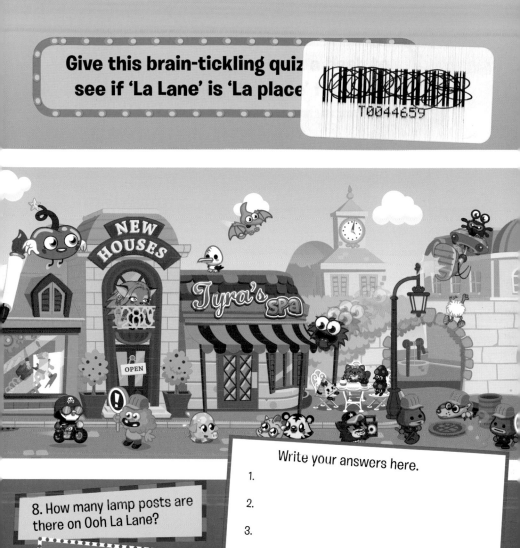

8. How many lamp posts are there on Ooh La Lane?

9. What colours are the canopies in front of Guiseppe's Ice-Scream Parlour and Tyra's Spa?

10. What is pictured on The Moshi Store shop sign?

Write your answers here.

1.

2.

3.

4.

5.

6

7.

8.

9.

10.

3

Print Workshop

Now's your chance to get your paws and fur really mucky! Grab some pens, pencils or paints down at the Print Workshop, and find that furry artist inside you. Who's your favourite? Better not shout it out too loud - you don't want to upset the others!

Diavlo

Poppet

Furi

Luvli

Zommer

Katsuma

4

Monstrous Mask

Be afraid, be very afraid! Nah, only kidding! Stick or copy this cool monster mask onto some card. If you know any sensible adults, get them to help you cut it out and tie some string through the holes, and then colour and decorate it. This is your chance to scare (or amuse!) your Moshi mates.

GROOOOWWWWLLL!

Ooh La Lane, What's Up?
Spot the Difference

Any monster worth their hairy socks knows that Ooh La Lane is one of the classiest places to hang out with your monster mates. But what's up today? Things aren't quite what they should be in da lane. Take a look and see if you can spot ten things that are out of place. Is the sinister Dr. Strangeglove behind this?

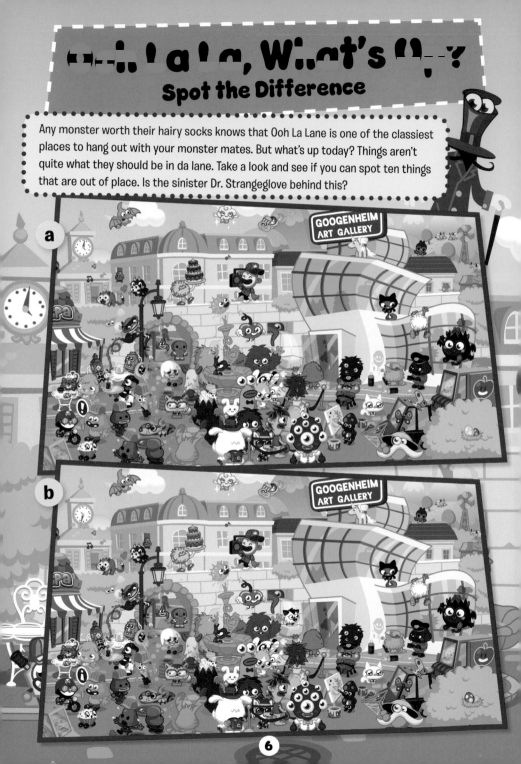

Tyra's
Spa Special

Even monsters need a little pampering every now and then. Put up your hairy paws and let Tyra work her magic . . . because you are worth it! And why not indulge in a bit of monster gossip with the queen of gossip herself while the Slop sets on your face?

Who else has come to the Spa for a splash of Goop! and a spray of Stink? Follow the wiggly lines to find out, then draw their face in the dressing table mirror. Put mud splats on them for a MUDlicious beauty treatment.

Ooh La Lane Word Search

Roary Scrawl is writing an article on Ooh La Lane for *The Daily Growl*. Of course, he has already got a lot of gossip, er, I mean, information from his girlfriend, Tyra, but he wants to interview a few other monsters as well. Find all the words in the grid below to help Roary with some ideas for his story.

Word list:
- SPA
- ICE-SCREAM
- GOOGENHEIM
- ART
- PRINT
- LAMP POST
- GIUSEPPE
- FOUNTAIN
- TYRA
- GOOP
- SLOP
- MOSHI
- HOUSES
- OOH LA LANE
- SKYSCRAPER

D	R	S	T	T	A	R	Y	T	G	L	O	T	E
M	S	P	R	F	Y	A	Y	L	M	T	N	H	M
V	K	A	D	S	H	G	I	D	O	I	Z	U	E
E	Y	S	B	W	K	O	S	E	R	L	E	J	P
N	S	R	H	U	E	O	U	P	C	L	O	N	P
A	C	Y	A	L	A	G	M	S	I	T	Y	F	E
L	R	N	O	T	I	E	U	U	E	P	O	L	S
A	A	I	S	D	P	N	L	R	G	S	Z	E	U
L	P	A	G	W	R	H	G	I	N	S	T	D	I
H	E	T	E	I	C	E	S	C	R	E	A	M	G
O	R	N	E	Q	R	I	M	P	N	H	L	Q	K
O	E	U	S	L	A	M	P	P	O	S	T	G	Y
Q	Y	O	N	K	X	E	M	L	W	O	R	G	O
H	E	F	R	M	O	S	H	I	C	R	G	W	L

A lamp post hugging, fluffy snuggler, has been spotted in La Lane. It shouldn't be hard to spot - its colour is in its name! If Roary can interview it, that will be a real Ooh La scoop. Unscramble the shaded letters in the grid to reveal the name of this little critter.

_ _ _ _ _ , _ _ _ _ _ _

Roy G. Biv's
Rainbow Sudoku

It's Roy G. Biv Day and that colourful rainbow rider, expert sky surfer and colossal cloud cruiser has cruised in to Ooh La Lane to spread his rainbow magic! Complete the Sudoku puzzle to make sure Monstro City has rainbows all year round. Remember, each of the six rainbow colours must only appear once in each horizontal and vertical line, and in each 6 x 6 box.

Art Lee's MonstART Gallery

Art Lee's MonstART art exhibition is an event not to miss in Ooh La Lane. Anyone who is anyone will be there. But what's this? Oh no, a glitterati disaster! That stinky ball of badness, Pirate Pong, has sneaked into the gallery and chopped bits out of the portraits. Quick, grab some sticky tape and help poor old Art Lee fix the paintings, before the opening night.

1 YSL NECHAC

2 RATAMA SLEAT

a
b
c
d
e
f

3 GENO YOGARNA

4 DELRE URIF

5 ZMIZ STONOS

6 PATICAN KUCB

Match the correct body or face parts to the six portraits on this page, and unscrabble the letters to reveal the names of the monsters on display.

Write your answers here.

1.   4.

2.   5.

3.   6

11

Guiseppe's Gelato

Ciao, piccoli mostri!* Quick, get your furry-selves down to the Ice-Scream parlour where that king of the gelatos, Giuseppe, is making a special ice cream for his first twenty customers. You can choose the toppings and treats to go on it - yummy! But hurry, you know how eager Giuseppe is to serve the next customer, and he might just tell you to scram before you've sunk your fangs into that dreamy, creamy dessert . . . hey, stop drooling, you're making the page wet!

*Hello, little monsters!

Chilly Code B. Cake.

Giuseppe does make a lickin' mean monster ice cream! The dreamy cold stuff reaches parts that even a bottle of Wobble-ade can't touch (unless your name is Roland Jones)! Now a certain not so SWEET monster, has been seen down at the parlour rather a lot recently. Break the ice-screamy code to find out his name and see why he is a regular at Giuseppe's.

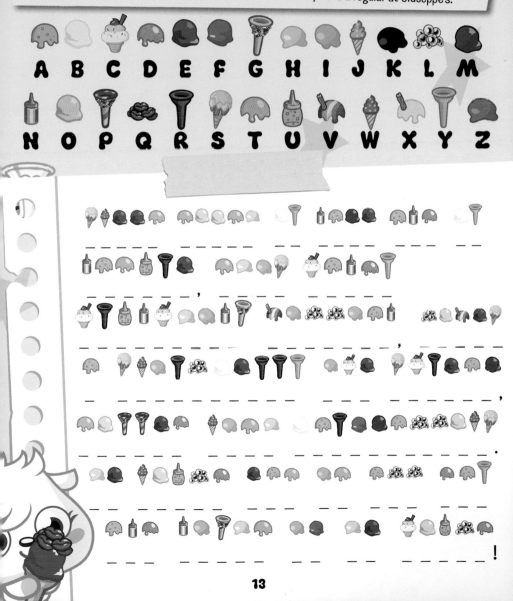

Where are the
Kitties and Puppies?

Tick the circles below when you find the Moshlings.

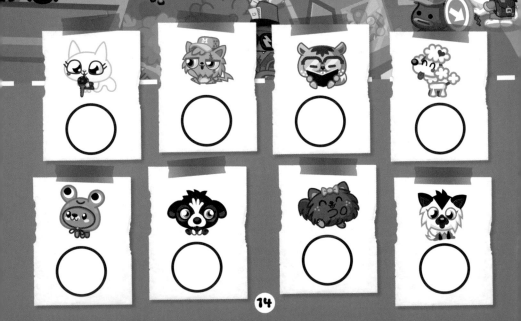